365 Interesting Facts
For Kids And Adults

365 Interesting Facts For Kids And Adults

Thrilling Fun Facts About Animals, Plants, History, And More. Every Day Read Interesting Facts For A Year.

Grace Henderson

The content contained within this book may not be reproduced, duplicated or transmitted without direct written permission from the author or the publisher.

Under no circumstances will any blame or legal responsibility be held against the publisher, or author, for any damages, reparation, or monetary loss due to the information contained within this book. Either directly or indirectly. You are responsible for your own choices, actions, and results.

Legal Notice:

This book is copyright protected. This book is only for personal use. You cannot amend, distribute, sell, use, quote or paraphrase any part, or the content within this book, without the consent of the author or publisher.

Disclaimer Notice:

Please note the information contained within this document is for educational and entertainment purposes only. All effort has been executed to present accurate, up to date, and reliable, complete information. No warranties of any kind are declared or implied. Readers acknowledge that the author is not engaging in the rendering of legal, financial, medical or professional advice. The content within this book has been derived from various sources. Please consult a licensed professional before attempting any techniques outlined in this book.

By reading this document, the reader agrees that under no circumstances is the author responsible for any losses, direct or indirect, which are incurred as a result of the use of the information contained within this document, including, but not limited to, — errors, omissions, or inaccuracies.

Table of Contents

1. Animals
1.1. Interesting aquatic animals

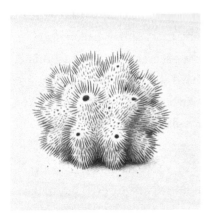

1. **Honeycomb bath sponge** is a natural filter that can clean 20 thousand times more water than its own volume just in one day! It is a primitive multicellular animal that mainly lives in the seas. It catches tiny particles, bacteria, and organic matter from the water, making the surrounding water cleaner. Thanks to this, sponges play an important role in maintaining the health of the marine ecosystem.

2. **Sea sponges were used by humans as far back as 3,000 years ago,** especially in ancient Greece, where they were used for bathing and hygiene. Due to their softness and ability to hold water, they became indispensable in everyday life and medicine of that time. It is one of the oldest natural means for cleansing and body care.

3. **Foam is a special kind of material that people make.** It's like a sea sponge, but it's made from chemicals. Foam has millions of tiny bubbles inside it, which makes it soft and bouncy. It can soak up lots of water or air, so it's perfect for things like furniture, sponges, and packaging. Foam is really handy because it is lightweight and can be shaped into any form.

4. **Sea sponges come in all sorts of colors,** from bright yellow to deep blue and red. They can be the size of a fingernail or several feet in diameter! Some kinds of sponges smell a little like the ocean. There are sea animals, like sea turtles, that like to eat sponges, but many sponges are poisonous. They can release a special disgusting juice to keep other animals away.

5. **Sea sponges are like the original survivors.** They've been around for over 600 million years and have survived numerous mass extinctions, making them some of the most resilient organisms on Earth.

6. **A coral reef is like an underwater city** built by tiny animals called coral polyps. They secrete calcium carbonate, forming hard skeletons. Reefs are found in warm, shallow parts of the ocean and can grow really big over time. Even though they cover only as much as 1% of the ocean, reefs are home to a quarter of all sea creatures! That makes them super important ecosystems.

7. **Coral reefs also protect our beaches from being washed away.** They help to slow down strong waves and storms before they reach the shore. This protects our beaches from being eroded and helps to prevent flooding and damage to coastal areas.

8. **Clownfish and sea anemones are the best friends!** They have a special relationship called symbiosis, in which they both benefit. Clownfish have a magic slime that keeps them safe from the anemones' stinging touch, so they can hide in the anemones' colorful tentacles and stay away from mean predators. Anemones are happy to have the clownfish around because they clean up their home by eating any nasty parasites and junk that get stuck on its tentacles. And sometimes, clownfish even share their food leftovers with anemones!

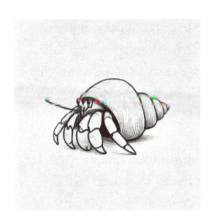

9. **Hermit crabs and sea anemones** are also great friends! The crab carries the anemone on its shell, and the anemone acts like a bodyguard, protecting the crab from predators with its stinging tentacles. In return, the anemone gets to travel around with the crab, which helps it find food more easily. The crab leaves behind leftovers that the anemone can eat.

10. **Jellyfish have been around for over 500 million years,** which makes them some of the oldest animals on Earth! Some kinds of jellyfish, like the immortal jellyfish, can even revert to a polyp stage, essentially turning back time! This means they can live forever, or so scientists think. But most jellyfish don't live that long. They get eaten by other sea creatures or get sick.

11. The Irukandji jellyfish is **one of the smallest measuring less than 0.4 inches** in diameter, and it's almost see-through! But other jellyfish can be really big. The giant Arctic jellyfish, or lion's mane jellyfish, can reach a bell diameter of up to 6.5 feet, with tentacles that may extend over 120 feet. Jellyfish come in all sorts of colors too, like pink, blue, and purple. Some jellyfish can even glow in the dark.

12. **Some jellyfish can be really dangerous.** The box jellyfish, for example, has a very strong sting that can cause severe pain, paralysis, and even stop your heart. Although it's not very common, most jellyfish aren't that dangerous. They just give you a little sting that might itch for a while.

13. **Cooperation between fish and jellyfish.** Some small fish like to hide among the tentacles of jellyfish. The jellyfish's stingers keep other fish away, so the little fish are safe. Sometimes, they even help the jellyfish by eating any parasites or leftover food that's stuck to its tentacles. It's a win-win situation!

14. **Physalia or Portuguese man-of-war might look like a jellyfish, but it's actually a colony of tiny animals living together.** Its bright blue or purple float helps it drift along the ocean. Its long, stinging tentacles can be over 100 feet long and are armed with stinging cells. If you get stung by one, it can hurt a lot. They're beautiful, but they're also very dangerous, although fatalities are rare.

15. **Mussels can filter and clean up to 10 gallons of water a day!** As they eat, they filter out tiny germs and dirt from the water, making it cleaner for everyone else. They contribute significantly to the health of aquatic ecosystems.

16. During World War II, Japanese soldiers **used special glowing shrimp** called Cypridina to see in the dark. These shrimp could make their own light because of special chemicals in their bodies. The soldiers would squeeze the shrimp to make them glow, and this gave off a soft light. This helped them read maps and letters without giving away their position with a regular flashlight.

17. Can you imagine a scorpion as big as a car? **Sea scorpions, or eurypterids, were giant sea creatures that lived millions of years ago.** They could grow up to 8 feet long! These scary-looking animals had big claws and lived in the ocean. They were top predators in the ocean, hunting fish and other sea creatures.

18. **Sperm whales are amazing divers!** They can dive really deep, down to **7,380 feet,** to find food like giant squids. That's almost a mile and a half down! No other mammal can dive as deep as they can.

1.2. Worms

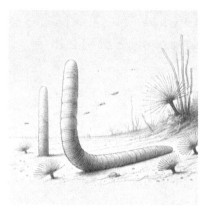

19. **Worms-siboglinidae** that live near deep-sea hydrothermal vents have a unique way of getting food. **They get their energy from special bacteria that live inside them**. These bacteria can turn chemicals like sulfur into food for the worm! So, these worms are basically eating chemicals, which helps them survive without light and usual food.

20. **Some worms**, like nematodes and ice worms (Hesiocaeca methanicola), **can survive in temperatures as low as 28.8°F,** which is the freezing point of seawater. They inhabit methane hydrates at the bottom of the ocean and can stay active even at these freezing temperatures. This allows them to live in conditions where most other organisms cannot survive.

21. **Did you know that some worms are really good parents?** Earthworms, for example, make special cocoons for their babies. The baby worms grow inside these cocoons, safe from any danger. There are also some sea worms, such as necklace worms that carry their eggs around on their bodies until they hatch! It's kind of like a worm backpack. Most worms don't do this, so it's pretty special.

22. **Flatworms,** such as planarians, **have an incredible ability to regenerate.** If you cut a flatworm in half, each part can grow into a completely new individual. Earthworms can also regenerate but to a lesser extent. They can regrow their tails if they lose them. This regenerative ability is an adaptation that helps these worms survive injuries and maintain their populations.

23. **Earthworms are super important for our gardens.** They dig tunnels underground, which helps to aerate the soil and let water in. They also eat dead leaves and plant stuff and poop out nutrients that plants need to grow. Can you believe that one earthworm can eat about 0.1 ounces of soil every day?

In a hectare of land, there can be up to a million earthworms, processing approximately 22,046 pounds of soil annually. This is equivalent to the work of a tractor, significantly improving soil structure and fertility.

1.3. Different colors of blood

24. **Red blood.** People and most animals have red blood. It's because of a special thing called hemoglobin. Hemoglobin has iron in it, and when it picks up oxygen, it turns bright red.

Blue blood. Octopuses and crabs have blue blood! This is because they have a special thing in their blood called copper. When copper meets oxygen, it turns blue.

Green blood: Some lizards have green blood! It's because they have a lot of special green stuff called biliverdin in their blood. Usually, our bodies get rid of this green stuff, but these lizards keep it, and it makes their blood green.

Purple blood. Some sea creatures have purple blood! It's because they have a special thing called hemerythrin in their blood. Hemerythrin helps them breathe and makes their blood look purple.

Clear blood. Some fish that live in really cold water have clear blood! That's because they don't need a lot of oxygen, so they don't need the red stuff in their blood.

1.4. Insects

25. **Spiders in Madagascar make one of the strongest kinds of silk in the world!** It's ten times stronger than steel of the same weight! In 2009, scientists collected silk from over a million spiders in Madagascar and made a special golden cloth. They showed the cloth in museums to show how amazing and strong spider silk can be.

26. **Termites make their homes from a strange mixture:** dirt, their own spit, and even their poop! These termite mounds are super strong and can grow up to 30 feet tall.

27. **The brightest fireflies in the world live in Central and South America**. They're called click beetles. These fireflies can shine so bright that you can see them from 100 feet away! They use this special light to find mates and to keep predators away.

28. In Africa, **people use termite mounds to build their homes,** make ovens for melting iron, and even to make roads and tennis courts! Termite mounds are really strong and can handle both hot and cold weather.

1.5. The most … animals

29. **Insects are the most diverse animals on Earth,** with over 1 million different kinds! That's more than all the fish and amphibians combined! Fish have about 34,000 kinds, and amphibians have around 8,000 kinds. So, insects are the biggest family of animals on our planet.

30. **The most jumpy ones.** Fleas are amazing jumpers! They can jump up to 8 inches high, which is about 150 times their own body length! If humans could jump as high compared to our size, we could jump over 900 feet, that's taller than most buildings!

31. Imagine living on top of a mountain so tall you can almost touch the sky! **Well, there's a tiny spider that does just that. It lives in the Himalayas, about 24,600 feet high!** It's one of the highest places any animal can be found. This spider eats tiny bugs that the wind carries up to its mountain home.

32. **There are worms as long as a football field!** The bootlace worm is the longest animal on Earth and it can grow to be over 180 feet long! These giant worms live in the oceans near Europe and like to hide in the sand or between rocks.

33. **Did you know that platypuses are one of the oldest mammals on Earth?** These unique animals have been around for about 120 million years and can only be found in Australia. What makes them really special is that they lay eggs, just like reptiles do. Most mammals give birth to live babies, so platypuses are very different!

34. **Can you believe that the biggest fish in the world is as big as a school bus?** The whale shark can grow up to 40 feet long and weigh as much as 20 tons! That's like having 4 elephants swimming around! Even though it's a giant, the whale shark is a gentle giant. It eats tiny little plants and animals called plankton, which it filters out of the water using its huge, 5-foot-wide mouth.

35. **The most dangerous shark to humans is the great white shark.** They can grow up to 20 feet long and weigh as much as 5,000 pounds! Great white sharks have very strong jaws that can give a really powerful bite. Sometimes they mistake people for seals, and that's why most shark attacks on humans happen. But don't worry, shark attacks are very rare, and sharks usually don't want to hurt people.

36. **The Goliath frog is the biggest frog in the world!** It can grow as big as 12.5 inches long, which is about the size of a small cat, and weigh up to 7.3 pounds! It's so big because it lives in Africa where there's lots of food like insects, small animals, and fish. All that food helps it grow really big compared to other frogs.

37. **The biggest seashell in the world comes from a giant clam called a giant clam.** These ocean shells can grow up to 4 feet long and weigh as much as 500 pounds! Giant clams live in warm waters in the Pacific and Indian Oceans and can live for over 100 years.

38. The peregrine falcon is the fastest bird in the world! When this falcon dives down to catch its prey, it can go as fast as 240 miles per hour! That makes it not only the fastest bird but the fastest animal on Earth. Peregrine falcons use their amazing speed to catch other birds while they're flying.

39. The cheetah is the fastest land animal! It can run up to 70 miles per hour over short distances, making it super speedy. But cheetahs can only run that fast for about 1,500 feet.

40. **The Komodo dragon is the biggest lizard in the world!** They can grow up to 10 feet long and weigh over 300 pounds! These lizards have very strong jaws and poisonous saliva that helps them kill their prey. Komodo dragons only live on a few islands in Indonesia, like Komodo Island, and they can hunt animals much bigger than them, like deer and even water buffalo.

1.6. Squids and shellfish

41. **Imagine a squid with eyes the size of a soccer ball! Giant squids can grow up to 43 feet long and have eyes that big!** They live in the dark, deep parts of the ocean, and their big eyes help them see in the dark, just like night-vision goggles.

42. **Giant squids and sperm whales have epic battles deep in the ocean.** Sperm whales are one of the few animals that hunt giant squids, and you can often find big scars on sperm whales from the squid's strong arms. Even though squids have powerful arms and suckers, sperm whales usually win because they are bigger and stronger, but it's a tough fight!

43. **Poisonous sea snails, like cone snails, live in warm waters of tropical and subtropical seas, including the Indian and Pacific Oceans.** Their beautiful shells hide a strong poison that they shoot out through their sharp teeth. The sting of some kinds can be deadly to humans, causing paralysis and breathing problems.

44. **Ever wondered how pearls are made?** Well, when a tiny grain of sand or something else gets stuck inside an oyster, it doesn't just sit there. The oyster doesn't like the feeling, so it starts to coat the grain with a shiny substance called nacre. Over many years, layer by layer, this creates a beautiful pearl.

People love pearls and use them to make jewelry, but collecting too many mollusks might lead to their extinction.

45. **People can make pearls.** It's called cultured pearl. They put a tiny thing inside an oyster's shell, and the oyster covers it with a shiny substance called nacre, just like it does in nature. We call these pearls cultured because they're grown on farms. This helps protect wild oysters and lets us get pearls in a safe way.

46. **Imagine a pearl as big as a small watermelon!** That's about how big the Pearl of Lao Tzu is. It weighs 14 pounds and was found in the Philippines. Another famous pearl is the Pearl of the South Seas, which weighs about 75 carats. These giant pearls are very special and important parts of history.

47. **Long ago, people used to get bright colors from special kinds of sea creatures, like snails.** One kind of snail, the marine gastropod mollusk, called a Murex, was used to make a very special purple color. This purple was called Tyrian purple, and it was so rare and hard to make that only very rich people, like kings and queens, could wear clothes dyed this color.

48. **Sea scallops have a pretty cool trick to stay safe.** When a scary fish or other animal comes near, they can quickly clap their shells together. This creates a jet of water that pushes them forward. It's like a tiny rocket! They can jump as far as 3 feet in one go, which is pretty impressive for something that doesn't swim very fast.

49. Cephalopods, such as squid, can jump out of the water. Flying squids are super cool sea creatures! They can actually jump out of the water and glide through the air like a bird. They can jump as high as 10 feet and travel up to 160 feet, using their fins to help them fly.

 It's a great way to escape from bigger fish that want to eat them. Imagine how surprised the sailors must have been when a giant squid jumped onto their boat in 1941!

50. Flying squids can leap out of the water at speeds of up to 25 miles per hour! They do this by shooting water out of their bodies, like a rocket, to get into the air. Then, they glide above the water, using their fins and arms to steer. It's a superfast way to escape from hungry fish and dolphins.

51. Squids are really smart for being animals without backbones! They have big brains and can do lots of cool things. For example, they can solve simple puzzles, change the color and pattern of their skin to hide, and even talk to each other using flashing lights. Some squids are really sneaky too! They can hide and wait for their food or work together as a team to catch it.

52. Squids have a cool trick to stay safe. When a scary animal is nearby, they can squirt out a cloud of ink. This ink makes a big mess in the water and confuses the other animals, like a magic trick! While the other animal is trying to figure out what happened, the squid can swim away as fast as it can. The ink can even have special chemicals that make the other animal's senses go numb, making it even harder for them to find the squid.

1.7. Sea stars

53. **Starfish have a really cool way of eating.** Instead of bringing their food into their mouths, they push their stomachs out of their mouths! They can reach their stomach out to cover their food, like clams or polyps, and digest it right there. Once the food is all eaten, they pull their stomach back inside.

54. **Too many starfish can be a big problem for the ocean.** For example, crown-of-thorns starfish can eat lots and lots of coral reefs. Coral reefs are like underwater cities for many sea animals. If too many starfish eat all the coral, many animals will lose their homes and food, and it can upset the whole underwater world.

55. Starfish are amazing creatures. If you cut off one of their arms, don't worry, it won't die! **Starfish can regrow their lost arms.** In some cases, if enough of the central part of the starfish is attached to the arm, a whole new starfish can grow from that arm!

1.8. Different kinds of fish

56. **Strange Fish. The Ocean Sunfish:** This is the heaviest bony fish in the world! It can weigh up to 5,000 pounds. It has a round, almost flat body that makes it look like a giant disc or a moon floating in the water.

57. **Meet the porcupine fish: A Spiky Surprise.** Porcupine fish are very interesting creatures. When they feel threatened, they can quickly fill their bodies with water, making themselves much bigger and rounder. At the same time, their skin is covered in sharp spines that stick out in all directions. This makes it very difficult for any other animal to swallow them.

58. **Strange Fish. The Seahorse:** A seahorse is a fish that looks like a chess piece! Its body is curved like an S, and it swims standing up. The coolest thing about seahorses is that the dads, not the moms, get pregnant. The female seahorse lays her eggs in a special pouch on the male's belly, and he carries the babies until they're ready to be born.

59. **Strange Fish. The Ragfish:** The ragfish has long, floppy fins that make it look like a piece of cloth or a seaweed leaf. This helps it hide from other animals among the corals and plants.

60. **The Coelacanth: A Living Fossil.** The coelacanth is a really special fish. People thought it had been extinct for 66 million years, but then in 1938, someone found a live one near South Africa! This "living fossil" can grow up to 6.5 feet long and weigh about 200 pounds.

Coelacanths are unique because their fins look a bit like legs, and scientists think they might be related to the ancient animals that first walked on land.

61. **Imagine a fish that can fly like a bird!** That's a flying fish! They live in warm oceans and can jump out of the water and glide for up to 650 feet using their big fins like wings! They do this to get away from bigger fish that want to eat them, like tuna and dolphins. But even though they can fly, they still have to watch out for hungry birds like albatrosses.

62. **The Mystery of the Eel.** For a long time, eels were a big mystery to scientists, especially when it came to how they had babies. For hundreds of years, people caught adult eels, but they never found any baby eels or eels that were about to have babies. Scientists finally figured out that eels live in European rivers for about 10 years without having babies. Then, they travel thousands of miles to the Sargasso Sea to have babies, but no one has ever seen them do it! After they have babies, the adult eels die, and the baby eels swim all the way back to Europe to grow up. It's amazing that even though scientists have been working on this puzzle for a long time, there are still some pieces missing.

63. **Fish Parents:** Some Care, Some Don't. Most fish have a simple way of having babies. They lay lots of eggs and then swim away. Some fish, like cod, can lay up to 9 million eggs in one season! These fish rely on having lots of babies to make sure some of them survive. But not all fish do this. Some fish, like the stickleback, are very good parents. The female stickleback lays fewer eggs, but the male stickleback builds a special nest for the eggs. He then guards the nest and fans the eggs with his fins to keep them healthy. When the baby fish hatch, he continues to look after them. So, even though he has fewer eggs, he makes sure his babies are safe.

1.9. Reptiles. Extinct and Modern

64. **Amazing Flying Frogs:** Flying frogs, also called gliding frogs, are really cool animals that live in the rainforests of Southeast Asia. They have special flaps of skin between their toes that they can spread out like wings. When they jump from tree to tree, they can glide for up to 50 feet! It's like they're flying! This helps them to avoid predators that live on the forest floor.

65. **From Water to Land: The Story of Reptiles.** A long, long time ago, about 315 million years ago, the first reptiles appeared on Earth. These animals evolved from amphibians, which were creatures that could live both in water and on land. However, reptiles were different. They had special scaly skin that kept them from drying out on land, and their eggs had tough shells so they could be laid on land, unlike amphibian eggs which needed water. This allowed reptiles to explore and live in many different land environments.

66. **Meet the Tuatara: A Dinosaur's Great Grandma.** The tuatara is a really ancient reptile that lives in New Zealand. It's been around for millions of years, even before the dinosaurs! Although it might look like a lizard, the tuatara is actually quite different. It's a "living fossil" because it hasn't changed very much over millions of years. Scientists study tuataras to learn more about how animals have changed over time.

67. **Giant Galapagos Tortoises.** Galapagos tortoises are some of the biggest and oldest tortoises in the world. They can grow up to 5 feet long and weigh as much as 500 pounds! They can live for over 100 years, and some even live to be 150 years old or more. They live on the Galapagos Islands and play an important role in the ecosystem by eating plants and spreading seeds. Because of their size and long lives, Galapagos tortoises

are a symbol of the Galapagos Islands and their unique wildlife.

68. **The Leatherback Sea Turtle:** A Giant of the Sea. Leatherback turtles are the biggest sea turtles in the whole world! They can grow up to 7 feet long and weigh over 2,000 pounds. Unlike other turtles, their shells aren't hard and bony. Instead, they have a tough, leathery shell that helps them dive really deep, up to 4,000 feet, to find food like jellyfish.

69. **Iguanas.** Iguanas are big lizards that live in hot, tropical places in America. They only eat plants. Some people think that raising iguanas could help solve the problem of not having enough food in these places. Iguanas grow quickly and are easy to take care of. Their meat is also very healthy and full of protein. In some countries, people already eat iguanas as part of their traditional food.

70. **Dinosaurs: Ancient Giants.** Dinosaurs were a group of reptiles that lived on Earth for over 160 million years. They first appeared about 230 million years ago and lived until about 65 million years ago. Dinosaurs came in all shapes and sizes, from giant ones like Tyrannosaurus Rex and Brachiosaurus to small ones about the size of a chicken. Some dinosaurs ate plants, and others were meat-eaters.

71. **Where Does the Word Dinosaur Come From?** The word "dinosaur" comes from two Greek words: "deinos," which means "terrible" or "fearful," and "sauros," which means "lizard." A long time ago, in 1842, a scientist named Richard Owen used this word to describe some strange bones he found. These bones were from animals that had lived millions of years ago. So, "dinosaur" literally means "terrible lizard,"

even though dinosaurs weren't really lizards.

72. Not All Dinosaurs Were Big. You might think that all dinosaurs were giant monsters, but that's not true! Some dinosaurs were really small. The smallest dinosaur we know of is called Microraptor. It was about the size of a crow! Microraptor was only about 2.5 feet long and weighed less than 2 pounds. It had feathers and could glide from tree to tree. That makes Microraptor one of the smallest and lightest dinosaurs ever found.

73. Gentleman's Fights. The marine iguanas on the Galapagos Islands have a special way of fighting. When male iguanas fight over territory or a mate, they don't bite or scratch. Instead, they have these special "pushing matches". They stand face-to-face, arch their backs, and then start pushing each other with their heads and bodies. It's like a contest to see who can push the other one over. Even though these fights can last a long time, the iguanas usually don't get hurt very badly.

74. The Water-Running Lizard. Have you ever heard of a lizard that can run on water? The basilisk is one of those amazing animals. With its big, flat feet and super-fast speed, it can create small air bubbles under its feet. These bubbles help it stay on top of the water as it runs for up to 15 feet. That's why people sometimes call it the "Jesus Christ lizard"!

75. Can You Train a Dragon? It's not very common, but people have been able to train Komodo dragons in zoos and wildlife parks. They can learn to do simple things like come when you call their name or follow you if you have food. Some trained dragons even let people pet them! It's pretty amazing because most lizards aren't very smart or friendly. Komodo dragons are special because they're very good at watching and learning new things.

1.10. Birds

76. Birds Use the Stars for Navigation. Scientists have figured out that birds can use the stars to find their way. In a special experiment, they put birds in a planetarium, which is like a big indoor sky. When they changed the stars, the birds tried to fly in a different direction! This shows that birds use the stars to help them know where to go when they migrate.

77. Arctic Terns: The Biggest Travelers. Arctic terns are amazing birds! They make the longest journey of any bird every year. They fly all the way from the Arctic to the Antarctic and back, which is about 25,000 miles! They follow the summer sun, so they see more daylight than any other animal on Earth. This long trip helps them find food and warm places all year round.

78. Birds Can Sleep While They Fly! Did you know that some birds can sleep while they're flying? Birds like swifts and petrels can take little "naps" where only half of their brain sleeps at a time. The other half stays awake to keep them flying and on track during their long journeys.

79. Swallows and Tunnels. Swallows are birds that fly to warm places for the winter. They used to fly over the big mountains called the Alps. But now, they're being smart! They've learned to fly through tunnels under the mountains. It's like taking a shortcut! They can even rest inside the tunnels on cars and other things. This helps them save energy for their long journey.

80. Ovenbirds are amazing builders! **They create their homes by mixing mud and dirt** with their spit to make strong, pot-shaped nests. These nests are so solid that they can weigh up to 10 pounds! They protect the birds from rain and keep other animals away. Some birds even use the same nest for many years!

81. **A Bird's Tiny Fortress.** The red ovenbird is like a tiny builder. It creates its home out of clay, and it's super strong! The nest can weigh as much as a small dog up to 15 pounds! It's like a little fortress for the baby birds, keeping them safe from the weather and predators.

82. **A Bird That Sews.** Tailorbirds are amazing! They can sew! They use spiderwebs or plant fibers to stitch leaves and grass together to make their nests. Their nests are shaped like small bags and hang from trees. These nests are a safe home for baby birds.

83. **Weaverbirds and Their Amazing Nests.** Weaverbirds are very colorful birds, often yellow and black. They are great at building nests! They weave grass and twigs together to make round or oval-shaped nests. These nests can be very heavy, up to 2 pounds! They hang the nests at the end of branches to keep baby birds safe from snakes and other animals.

84. **Eurasian penduline tit** is a small bird that builds very special nests. These nests are shaped like little bags, and they're made of soft materials like fluff and fur. They can weigh up to a whole pound! Tits often hang their nests over water on trees to keep them safe from other animals.

85. **A Bird's Saliva House.** Swiftlets are birds that build their homes out of their own saliva! That's right, their spit! They live in warm places like Southeast Asia and stick their nests to rocks and caves. These nests are so strong they can weigh up to 3 ounces! People collect these nests to make a special soup. It's considered a delicacy and is very expensive.

86. **The Megapode's Big Nest.** Australian megapodes, or mound-builders, are like nature's engineers! They make huge nests out of leaves, grass, and sand. These nests can be as wide as 10 feet and as tall as 3 feet! They carefully watch the temperature inside the nest and add or take away materials to keep it just right. This helps their eggs hatch perfectly.

87. **Cliff-Dwelling Birds.** Guillemots are birds that live on cliffs. They don't build nests like other birds. Instead, they lay their eggs directly on the rocky ledges. Their eggs have a special pear shape. This shape helps the eggs stay on the cliff, even if there's a strong wind. They spin around instead of rolling in a straight line.

88. **The Giant Moa.** The moa was a huge bird that couldn't fly. It lived in New Zealand. These birds were as tall as a two-story house! They weighed as much as a refrigerator! But sadly, they don't exist anymore. They died out about 500 years ago.

89. **The Fastest Runner.** Ostriches are the biggest birds on Earth. They can grow up to 9 feet tall and weigh over 300 pounds. Even though they're too heavy to fly, ostriches are amazing runners. They can run faster than a race car!

90. **Penguins can't fly, but they're amazing swimmers!** They use their wings like flippers to swim really fast. They can swim up to 15 miles per hour underwater!

1.11. Marsupial animals

91. **A Pocket for Babies.** Marsupials, like kangaroos and koalas, have a special pocket on their tummy called a pouch. When their babies are born, they're very small and not fully developed. The baby crawls into the pouch where it's safe and can drink its mom's milk. It stays in the pouch until it's big enough to leave the pouch and live on its own.

92. **Kangaroos can only hop forward!** Because of their strong back legs and long tails, they can't hop back.

93. **Koalas eat almost only eucalyptus leaves.** Even though these leaves are poisonous to most animals, koalas have a special body that can handle the poison. Eucalyptus leaves aren't very nutritious, but they have lots of water in them, so koalas don't need to drink as much.

94. **The Tasmanian wolf, also called a thylacine, was a meat-eating animal with a pouch.** It lived in Tasmania, Australia, and New Guinea. It looked a bit like a dog with stripes on its back, which is why people sometimes called it a Tasmanian tiger. Sadly, the last Tasmanian tiger died in a zoo in 1936, and now they are all gone.

95. **Have you heard of the Tasmanian devil?** It's a small animal from Tasmania that carries its babies in a pouch. Even though it's small, it's very strong and has a really loud scream. Its jaws are so powerful that it can crush bones!

1.12. Mammals

96. **Whales and dolphins might look like big fish, but they're actually mammals.** That means they breathe air with their lungs, just like us. They have a special hole on top of their heads called a blowhole. When they need air, they swim to the surface and breathe out through their blowhole. Some whales, like sperm whales, can dive really deep into the ocean to find food. They can go down as far as 7,380 feet and stay underwater for almost an hour and a half!

97. **Did you know that scientists have been looking at dolphins to build better boats?** Dolphins have special skin that helps them glide through the water really fast. By studying dolphin skin, scientists have been able to create special coatings that make boats and torpedoes go faster and smoother through the water.

98. Back in the late 1800s, when people were first putting underwater cables across the ocean, there was a big problem with **giant sperm whales**! These huge sea creatures would dive super deep looking for food and sometimes get all tangled up in the cables! They might think they were yummy snacks or just get stuck. It was one of the first surprises people had when they started putting cables in the ocean.

99. **Dolphins are really good friends!** If one dolphin gets hurt or sick, the others will help keep it at the surface so it can breathe. They also work together to find food and protect each other from scary animals like sharks.

100. During the Gulf War, dolphins were used to find and clear away underwater bombs, called mines. Dolphins can use a special power called echolocation to see things underwater, even if it's dark or murky. They helped soldiers find the mines safely so that they could be made harmless, keeping the divers out of danger.

101. Pangolins are nature's little tanks! Covered in scales, they can roll up into a ball so tight, not even a lion could unroll them. These scaly critters love to eat ants and termites, and they use their super long, sticky tongues to slurp them up.

102. Elephants are some of the smartest animals on Earth! They can even recognize themselves in a mirror, which shows they know who they are. Elephants have amazing memories and can remember places with food and water for many years. They can feel sad or happy, just like us. And when one of their friends dies, they have special ceremonies to show how much they care.

103. Chimpanzees are really smart, they're almost as smart as a 5-year-old kid. They can remember numbers in order, solve puzzles, and even learn sign language. Some chimpanzees are even better than people at remembering things for a short time!

104. Platypuses have a super cool power, their beaks can sense tiny electric signals from the animals they hunt, even underwater. It's like having a built-in metal detector for finding food, even with their eyes closed!

105. **Taming zebras was really hard** because they're much wilder and harder to predict than horses. But in the early 1900s, people tried to use zebras to pull carriages, especially in Africa where they're less likely to get sick than horses. A famous explorer named Lord Walter Rothschild even tamed some zebras and drove them around London to show that it could be done.

106. **The Steller's sea cow was a huge sea animal.** It could grow as long as a school bus and weigh as much as 10 elephants! It lived in cold waters near Russia and ate seaweed. Sadly, the Steller's sea cow was hunted until there were none left. People killed them for their meat and fat. It only took 27 years after it was discovered in 1741 for this amazing animal to disappear forever.

2.Plants

2.1. Interesting facts about plants

107. The plant world is huge! **There are about 390,000 different types of plants out there.** That's a lot!! Most of them have flowers, but there are also some really cool ones like mosses, ferns, and big, tall pine trees.

108. **Did you know that plants are like tiny air cleaners**? They use sunlight to turn bad air (carbon dioxide) into good air (oxygen). Most of the oxygen we breathe comes from the ocean and forests. It takes about 2,000 years for all the oxygen on Earth to be replaced, and plants do all the work!

Plants make their own food. They use sunlight, water, and air to create food called glucose. It's like cooking, but plants do it with sunlight. All living things, including us, need to eat plants or animals that eat plants, so plants are really important!

109. **Plants have a special trick to get more sunlight.** When one side of a plant doesn't get enough light, it grows faster on that side. This makes the plant lean towards the sun, so all the leaves can get enough light to grow big and strong.

110. **The stem of a plant is really important.** It holds up the leaves and flowers, and it carries water and food from the roots to the rest of the plant. The longest stems belong to vines like rattan, which can grow up to 650 feet long!

111. Flowers bloom for different lengths of time. A dandelion flower is open for just a few days, but a rafflesia flower, one of the largest flowers in the world, can stay open for about a week. There are also some plants, like the night-blooming cereus cactus, whose flowers open for only one night before they start to wilt.

112. Get ready to be amazed! The **Victoria amazonica** is a giant water lily with leaves so big, they can hold a child. That's like having your own personal lily pad! You can find these incredible plants in the Amazon River.

113. Joseph Paxton looked at a giant water lily leaf and got a great idea! **He used the way the leaf was built to design the Crystal Palace in London in 1851.** The leaf has strong, lightweight ribs, and Paxton used that idea to make the Crystal Palace out of iron and glass. It was strong and light, just like the leaf!

2.2. Ancient plants

114. One of the most famous forests in the world is made of stone! It's called the Petrified Forest and it's in Arizona, USA. These trees are about 225 million years old! They turned into rock because of volcanoes. You can see whole tree trunks that are now made of colorful minerals like quartz.

115. Can you believe that **ferns** were on Earth before dinosaurs? They're really ancient plants! Over 360 million years ago, ferns were the biggest plants around. Back then, the air was full of oxygen and some ferns were as tall as a 10-story building. Today, we find these old ferns as coal, which we burn to get energy.

2.3. Carnivorous plants and parasitic plants

116. **Carnivorous plants** like Venus flytraps and sundews love to eat bugs. Since they live in places with poor soil, they have to get creative to find food. They use cool traps, like sticky leaves or snapping jaws, to catch insects. Once they have a bug, they use special juices to digest it and get important things like nitrogen.

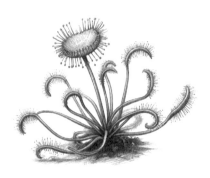

117. **Sundews** catch insects with tiny, sticky droplets on their leaves that look like dewdrops. When a bug lands on the leaf, it gets stuck. Then, the plant slowly wraps its leaves around the bug and digests it with special juices. It's cool how sundews can slowly move their leaves to catch bugs, even though they look still.

118. **Nepenthes** are meat-eating plants with special cups that catch insects and small animals. There's a special liquid inside the cup that digests the bugs. Some Nepenthes can even catch tiny frogs or even small rats!

119. **Mistletoe is a plant that lives on other trees.** It's like a plant vampire! It takes water and food from the tree it's growing on. Even though it's a parasite, mistletoe has beautiful white berries that birds love to eat and its pretty flowers attract bugs that help plants make more flowers and berries. Mistletoe also flowers in winter when other plants are sleeping.

120. **There's a fun tradition that says you have to kiss someone if you're standing under the mistletoe!** It's an old custom, especially popular in Europe and America. People believe that mistletoe is a lucky plant that brings love. So if you're under a mistletoe during a holiday like Christmas, you're supposed to kiss to bring good luck and make your relationship stronger.

121. **One of the most famous parasitic plants is the rafflesia.** This plant doesn't have a stem or leaves, and it needs to live on another plant to get food. Rafflesia is famous for its giant flower, which can be as big as 3 feet across and weigh up to 15 pounds! But here's the weird part: it smells like rotten meat to attract flies to help it make more flowers.

2.4. Trees

122. **Sequoias or redwoods are the tallest trees in the world.** They can grow over 380 feet tall, which is taller than the Statue of Liberty! These giants can live for over 2,000 years and grow on the west coast of the United States. Redwoods have thick bark that protects them from fire and disease, helping them live so long.

123. Can you imagine eating dinner inside a tree? Well, back in the middle of the 20th century, people in California did just that! They built **a small restaurant inside a huge redwood tree** that was hollow. It was like eating in a treehouse, but much bigger! These kinds of restaurants are closed now to keep the redwoods safe.

124. **Ginkgo biloba is one of the oldest trees on Earth!** It's been around for over 200 million years. People call it a "living fossil" because it hasn't changed much since the time of the dinosaurs. Ginkgo biloba has special fan-shaped leaves, and it's used in medicine to help people remember things better and improve their blood flow.

125. **Imagine a tree that can store enough water to fill a swimming pool! That's a baobab tree!** They have super thick trunks that hold tons of water to help them survive when it doesn't rain. Baobabs look a bit strange as if they were planted upside down! Their branches look like roots! They're really old too, some can live for 2,000 years! Animals and people in Africa depend on baobab trees for food and water.

126. **Bottle trees** got their name because their trunks are really thick and wide, just like a bottle! Like baobab trees, they can store water in their trunks to survive when there's no rain. Bottle trees grow in Australia and can hold up to 1,000 liters of water, keeping them safe from the hot sun.

127. **The biggest leaves in the world belong to a type of palm tree called a raffia palm.** Raffia palm leaves can grow up to 80 feet long! These giant leaves are used by people who live nearby to make roofs and other things.

128. **Corypha or Talipot Palm** has really big leaves that look like giant umbrellas! These leaves can be as wide as 16 feet across. People who live nearby use them to make roofs for their houses, boats, and even umbrellas!

129. **Cariota or the fishtail palm** got its name because its leaves look like a fish's tail! The sap from this palm can make your skin feel itchy, so it's also called "stinging". These palms are also special because people use their trunks to make palm sugar.

130. **Breadfruit can weigh up to 10 pounds** and taste like potatoes or bread when they're cooked. These fruits are really important food in hot countries. One tree can grow up to 200 fruits a year, which is enough to feed a whole family!

43

131. **Coco de mer nuts** are the biggest nuts in the whole world! They can weigh up to 66 pounds and look like two coconuts put together. These special nuts only grow on the Seychelles Islands and are protected by law because they're so rare and valuable.

132. **In autumn, leaves change color** because trees are getting ready for winter. During this time, they stop making chlorophyll, which is the green stuff that helps plants get energy from the sun. When the green goes away, we can see other colors like yellow and orange carotenoids, and red anthocyanins.

2.5. Seaweed

133. **Seaweed is a simple plant** that lives in water and can make oxygen through photosynthesis. They come in all sorts of sizes, from tiny ones you can't see to giant ones like kelp, which can grow up to 200 feet long! Seaweed is super important for our planet because it makes up about 70% of all the oxygen on Earth.

134. **Laminaria, brown seaweed,** or kelp lives in cold water and can grow as deep as 100 feet! It likes the water to be between 32°F and 68°F and lives in the northern oceans. Kelp grows really fast and makes millions of tiny seeds called spores that grow into new kelp plants.

135. **Seaweed, especially kelp, helps protect Santa Barbara Harbor from big storms.** These seaweeds make underwater "forests" that slow down the waves and keep them from damaging the shore and the harbor.

136. Have you ever seen a sea that's actually red? **The Red Sea got its name because of tiny seaweed.** When they grow really fast, they can make the water look reddish or brownish. It's like the sea is blushing!

137. Plankton is tiny little creatures that float around in the water. They're like the start of the food chain in the ocean. There are two kinds: **phytoplankton**, which are like tiny plants that make oxygen, and **zooplankton**, which are tiny animals. Plankton are super important for life in the ocean because lots of sea animals, from small fish to big whales, eat them.

138. Some tiny plants called single-cell algae **can live in super-hot places,** like hot springs and geysers! These special algae, called thermophilic cyanobacteria, can even live in water that's almost boiling! They make the water and rocks look really colorful, like green, yellow, and orange.

139. **Have you ever seen red rain?** It might sound scary, but it's actually caused by tiny plants called algae. These algae have a red color, and when there are a lot of them, they can make the rain look red. It's like a magic trick, but it's all natural!

140. Imagine a forest that floats on the water! **Sargassum seaweed makes these amazing underwater forests.** They don't need to be planted; they just float around. These floating forests are home to lots of cool sea creatures. Sargassum is like a big, floating apartment building for ocean animals. Sargassum plays an important role in marine ecology.

2.6. Mushrooms

141. **Mushrooms aren't plants or animals.** They're in a whole different group called fungi. Unlike plants, they can't make their own food from sunlight. Instead, they get food by breaking down things like dead leaves or old logs. Fungi are pretty cool because they're kind of a mix between plants and animals, but they're their own special group.

142. **There are about 10,000 kinds of mushrooms that you can eat,** but people only pick and eat a few hundred of them. On the other hand, there are about 100 kinds of mushrooms that are poisonous and can make you very sick, or even kill you.

143. **The death cap** mushroom is one of the most dangerous poisonous mushrooms in the world. It looks like a normal, safe mushroom. Even eating just a tiny bit of a death cap can make you very, very sick and can even kill you if you don't get help right away.

144. Ever heard of a truffle? It's like a hidden treasure! **These special mushrooms grow underground and are really hard to find.** Dogs and pigs can sniff them out because they have a strong smell. Chefs use them to make super delicious food that's really fancy.

145. Have you ever seen a flower that looks like several fingers? There are some weird mushrooms called "Devil's Fingers" that look like that! They start out as a little ball, but then they open up like a flower and show bright red spooky-looking fingers. Even though they're kind of cool to look at, they smell really gross! The smell helps insects find them, and the insects help the mushroom spread its seeds.

146. Have you ever seen a mushroom that can crawl? Slime molds are like tiny, oozy animals that can move! They look like blobs and they slowly slide along the ground. Slime molds love to eat bacteria and other tiny things. It's like they're going on a treasure hunt to find their next meal! Most mushrooms can't move at all, so slime molds are really special.

2.7. Lichens

147. Lichens are a partnership between a fungus and an algae (or cyanobacteria). The fungus provides protection and moisture for the algae, while the algae uses photosynthesis to create food for both organisms. This unique partnership allows lichens to survive in extreme environments, such as on bare rocks, tree bark, and in arctic regions.

148. Lichens are some of the oldest living organisms on Earth. Some species can live for over a thousand years! Due to their ability to survive in extreme conditions, lichens can be found in places where other organisms cannot, such as the Arctic, Antarctica, and the highest mountain peaks.

149. **Some lichens, like the Cladonia lichen,** look really strange! They kind of look like tiny reindeer antlers or coral from the ocean.

150. **Another cool lichen is called Parmelia.** It has special colors that make it glow when you shine a special kind of light on it!

2.8. Mosses

151. **Mosses are some of the oldest plants on Earth!** They've been around for over 400 million years! Mosses are really tough and can grow in lots of different places, even in very cold or hot places. They can also soak up lots of water, like tiny sponges!

152. **Mosses are super cool because they can dry out almost completely and still be alive!** It's like they can go to sleep for a really long time. Some mosses can stay asleep for years, or even decades! When it rains, they wake up and start growing again. It's amazing how tough they are!

153. **Sphagnum moss is like a super sponge!** It can soak up water that's 20 to 25 times heavier than it is! So, if you have a dry piece of sphagnum moss that weighs 1 ounce, it can soak up so much water that it will weigh up to 25 ounces! That's why it's great for soaking up spills.

2.9. Plant cooperation (symbiosis)

154. Did you know that trees and fungi can be best friends? This special friendship is called mycorrhiza. The fungi help the tree roots get more water and yummy nutrients from the soil. In return, the tree gives the fungi some of the food it makes from sunlight. It's like a friendship where everyone helps each other!

155. Orchids start their lives with a little help from their fungi friends! Orchid seeds are so small and don't have any food stored inside them. To grow, they need a special kind of fungus to help them out. The fungus gives the orchid seed the food it needs to start growing.

156. Myrmecodia is a special plant that has a home for ants inside it! The plant has hollow stems and roots where the ants can build their nest. The ants like living there because it's a safe place. In return for a home, the ants protect the plant from bad bugs and give it yummy food. They leave their food scraps inside the plant, which helps the plant grow.

157. **Some tiny creatures called amoebas and paramecia have tiny plants living inside them.** These plants make food and oxygen for the amoebas and paramecia using sunlight. In return, the amoebas and paramecia keep the plants safe and give them food. It's like a tiny house where the plants and animals help each other out!

2.10. Flowers

158. Roses are one of the oldest flowers we know about. There's a rose bush in Germany that's almost 1,000 years old! It's really old! This rose bush grows near a church and still blooms every year, even though it's so old.

159. Roses come in all sorts of colors! You can find red roses, pink roses, white roses, yellow roses, orange roses, and even purple ones. There are also special black and blue roses, but the "black" ones are really dark red, and the "blue" ones are made by scientists through special breeding.

160. People used to call Persia "the land of roses and nightingales." Roses were very important in Persian culture. They had beautiful gardens filled with roses. Persians thought roses were a symbol of beauty and love. Poets would write poems about roses, and nightingales would sing beautiful songs in the rose gardens. Together, the roses and nightingales were symbols of romance and the beauty of nature.

161. Have you ever wondered where the word "rose" came from? Well, it might be connected to an ancient name for Syria! Syria was called "Suri" or "Suriana" many years ago. People in Syria were really good at growing roses. Some people think that when people traded roses and rose oil from Syria to other countries, they also shared the name "rose" with everyone.

162. **Wars of the Roses.** In England, a long time ago in the 1400s, there was a big war between two families, the Lancasters and the Yorks. They both wanted to be the royal family and rule the country. The Lancasters had a red rose as their symbol, and the Yorks had a white rose. After many years of fighting, Henry Tudor, who was a Lancaster, won. He married someone from the York family to unite the two families. To remember this, they created a new symbol called the Tudor rose, which had both red and white parts.

163. **Can you imagine a flower so small you need a magnifying glass to see it?** The world's smallest flower belongs to a tiny plant called Wolffia. These little green plants float on water and are only about 0.02 inches across! They don't even have stems or leaves, and their flowers are so tiny you can hardly see them.

164. **The Titan Arum, or "corpse flower," is one of the tallest flowers in the world.** It can grow up to 10 feet tall! It has a really stinky smell, like rotten meat, which helps it attract bugs to help it grow. This flower doesn't bloom very often, maybe only once every 7-10 years.

165. In the 17th century, there was a crazy thing called **"Tulip Mania"** in the Netherlands. People were obsessed with tulips! They bought and sold tulip bulbs, and the prices kept going up and up until they were super expensive. Some people even traded away their houses for just one tulip bulb! But then, suddenly, the prices crashed, and many people lost all their money. It was like a big bubble that popped!

166. If you want a flower that keeps blooming and blooming, **Vanilla or the vanilla orchid** is a good choice. It can bloom for many months. But if you really want a long-lasting flower, **the anthurium** is the winner! It can bloom for up to 6-8 months straight without stopping! It's like a never-ending flower show.

2.11. Names of states and plants

167. **Have you ever heard of a plant called maguey?** It's a really important plant in Mexican history! The people who lived in Mexico before the Spanish arrived, called the Aztecs, used maguey for almost everything. They ate it, drank it, and even made clothes from it! In fact, the name "Mexico" might come from an Aztec god named Mexitl who was connected to the maguey plant.

168. **Grenada is named after a fruit called a pomegranate.** In Spanish, pomegranate is "granada". Pomegranates were a symbol of fertility and beauty.

169. **Barbados got its name from the Portuguese word "Los Barbados"**, which means "bearded". This is because there were a lot of fig trees on the island that had roots hanging down, making them look like they had beards!

170. **The name "Guatemala" might come from the word "Cuauhtēmallān",** which means "place of many trees" in an old language called Nahuatl. It's because Guatemala had a lot of forests a long time ago.

2.12. Forests

171. Imagine a forest so big, it's like a whole other world. That's **the Amazon rainforest!** It's the biggest rainforest on our planet and it's found in South America. This amazing forest makes a lot of the air we breathe. In fact, this giant forest produces about 20% of the oxygen we breathe.

172. **Costa Rica's cloud forests** are special because they're always covered in a blanket of clouds. This makes them a perfect home for lots of cool plants and animals that you can't find anywhere else, like beautiful orchids and really small frogs.

173. If you were to visit Canada, you'd see a lot of trees! In fact, **Canada has the largest forests in all of North America.** These forests, called boreal forests, cover about 60% of Canada. They're really important for our Earth's climate.

174. Have you heard of the **Lacandon Jungle?** It's a big rainforest in Mexico. It's one of the last big ones in North America. This jungle is home to so many different kinds of plants and animals, and some of them you can't find anywhere else in the world.

175. In rainforests, there are plants called **epiphytes.** They grow on other plants, but they don't hurt them! For example, orchids and bromeliads grow on tree branches to get more sunlight.

176. **In rainforests, vines can grow up to 200 feet long!** These plants climb up trees to reach the sunlight. They use the trees like ladders.

177. **The cacao tree, which gives us chocolate, only grows in rainforests.** The cacao pods grow right on the tree trunk, which is kind of weird for a tree!

178. Can you believe that rainforests, which are only about **7% of our planet, are home to more than half of all the plants and animals** in the world? That's a lot of living things in one place!

2.13. Prairies, savannas, deserts

179. Grasslands, like **prairies and steppes, cover about 40% of the Earth's land.**

180. Did you know that **bamboo** is actually a type of grass? It's the tallest grass in the world and can reach heights of 100 feet! What's even crazier is that it can grow up to 3 feet in a single day. That's super-fast!

181. **Imagine a giant green playground filled with tall grass and a few trees.** That's a savanna! These places are like giant snack bars for animals like elephants and zebras because there's so much yummy grass to munch on.

182. **Savannas cover about 20% of the Earth!** You can find them mostly in Africa, South America, and Australia. Savannas have two big seasons: a dry season and a rainy season.

183. Savannas are home to some of the biggest animals on Earth, like **elephants, giraffes, rhinos, and lions**. They're all really good at living in grassy places.

184. If you go to a savanna, you'll see **acacia and baobab trees.** These trees are spread out because the soil in savannas isn't very rich. It can't support a lot of trees growing close together.

185. **Most of the biggest grasslands in the world are in Africa.** Countries like Kenya and Tanzania have huge areas covered in tall grasses, which we call savannas.

186. **Prairies** are big, grassy plains. You can find them mostly in **North America, especially in the United States and Canada.** They're covered in lots of tall and short grasses.

187. Prairies are known for their strong winds and big changes in temperature. It can be very cold in the winter and very hot in the summer. Animals like **bison and coyotes** are used to these tough conditions.

188. Deserts are home to special plants called **cacti.** These plants store water inside their stems, so they can survive even when it doesn't rain for a long time. A saguaro cactus can hold as much as 200 gallons of water!

189. The Sahara Desert is really big! It's about **3.6 million square miles,** which makes it the biggest hot desert in the world. The hottest it's ever been in the Sahara was **136 degrees Fahrenheit** in a place called El Azizia, Libya, in 1922.

190. **You might think a desert is always hot and full of sand, but that's not always true!** A desert is any place that gets very little rain, snow, or even fog — less than 10 inches in a whole year. The biggest desert on Earth is actually the Antarctic, which is super cold and covered in ice. It gets less than 2 inches of snow every year! The Sahara is the biggest hot desert, but it's not the biggest desert overall.

191. **Tamarix and camelthorn plants live in the desert.** They have super long roots that go way down into the ground to find water.

192. There are some amazing plants in the desert, like the **welwitschia**. They can live for hundreds of years! They don't need a lot of water to survive, just a little bit of rain or morning dew is enough.

193. Did you know that **oleander** is one of the few plants that can bloom in the desert? It has thick, leathery leaves that help it hold onto its water, so it can survive in hot, dry places.

2.14. Swamps

194. **Swamps** are wet, soggy places where water sits on or just below the ground. This makes it a great place for plants like reeds and mosses to grow. Swamps cover about 6% of the Earth. 201. You can find swamps all over the world, from hot and humid places to cold and icy ones.

For example, the Great Swamp is in the United States, and there are big swamps in the Amazon rainforest too.

195. Swamps are one of the most important places on Earth. They help slow down climate change by trapping a lot of carbon dioxide, a gas that makes our planet warmer.

196. In **some swamps, you can find a special kind of soil called peat.** Peat is made from plants like moss that have been slowly decaying for many years. People use peat to burn in fireplaces or to help plants grow in gardens.

197. **Bog bodies** are people who lived a long, long time ago and were found in swamps in northern Europe. The special conditions in the swamps, like the cold and no air, helped to keep these bodies from decaying. **The Tollund Man** is a really famous bog body, and he's almost 2,400 years old!

198. **Swamps are like time capsules.** People have discovered very old weapons, tools, and jewelry in great condition in swamps. The wet and airless environment of swamps helps to preserve things for thousands of years.

199. Sometimes, when people dig in swamps, they find **big chunks of peat.** Inside these chunks, there can be pieces of old plants and animals that have been trapped there for a long, long time. Scientists study these pieces to learn about what the world was like a long time ago.

3. Geography

200. Have you ever seen a giant space rock? **The Hoba Meteorite is one!** It fell to Earth in Namibia, near Grootfontein. It weighs a whopping 120,000 pounds and is about 9 feet long, 9 feet wide, and 3 feet thick. Most of it is made of iron and some nickel. Scientists think it is about 80,000 years old!

201. **The North Pole is a very unique spot on our planet.** If you were at the North Pole, it would feel like the Earth isn't spinning at all. That means there's no sunrise or sunset, and you wouldn't be able to tell which way is north, south, east, or west. Every direction would look like south!

202. **At the equator, the day and night are always the same length:** 12 hours each. Twice a year, in spring and fall, the sun is directly overhead at noon. We call this "the sun is at its zenith," and it happens in March and September.

203. **The Samoa Islands were discovered in the 18th century.** A Dutch explorer, Jacob Roggeveen, was the first European to see them in 1722. But he thought they were part of Tonga! A French explorer, Louis Antoine de Bougainville, made the same mistake. It wasn't until more exploring was done in 1824 that people realized Samoa was its own place.

204. **The Four Corners is a special place in the United States** where four states meet: Arizona, Utah, Colorado, and New Mexico. It's the only place in the whole country where you can stand in four states at once! There's a special marker there, and people love taking pictures of themselves standing in different states all at the same time.

205. **The Diomede Islands** are two small islands in the Bering Strait. They're only 2.5 miles apart, but they're in different countries and have very different times. The western island, called Ratmanov, belongs to Russia. The eastern island, called Krusenstern, belongs to the United States. There's an imaginary line between them called the International Date Line. That means that when it's Saturday morning at 6 AM on the American island, it's actually Sunday morning at 9 AM on the Russian island! It's like stepping into a time machine!

206. If you were looking for a country with lots of islands, you'd want to visit **Indonesia, the Philippines, or Japan.** Indonesia has the most, with over 17,000 islands! The Philippines comes next with around 7,000 islands, and Japan isn't far behind with over 6,800 islands. It's amazing to think about how many islands these countries have. They're like giant puzzle pieces floating in the ocean! These countries are really special because they have so many islands.

207. Did you know that **France** shares a border with Brazil? It's true! France has a part of its country called French Guiana, which is in South America, right next to Brazil. So while most people think of France as a European country, it's actually much bigger than you might think. Instead of just being neighbors with countries like Belgium and Germany, France is also neighbors with Brazil and its big rainforests!

208. **The equator is an imaginary line that divides the Earth** into the Northern and Southern Hemispheres. It goes through 13 different countries, like Ecuador, Brazil, Congo, Kenya, and Indonesia. These countries have really cool rainforests and lots of different plants and animals. Since they're right on the equator, the weather is pretty much the same all year round!

209. **The Marble Canyon** in the Grand Canyon got its name because it has a really thick layer of marble, over a thousand feet thick! This big slab of marble is so shiny and smooth that it looks like glass. For many, many years, water and wind have been polishing it, making it look really cool and sparkly. When the sunlight hits it, it shines in all sorts of colors, making the canyon walls look amazing.

210. Not far from Canada, in the Atlantic Ocean, there's an island called **Sable Island**. It's sometimes called the "Graveyard of the Atlantic" because so many ships have sunk there! It's shaped like a big crescent moon and is about 26 miles long. This island is always moving because of the ocean waves. It's actually moving to the east over 650 feet every year! Over 350 ships have crashed there, which is why it's so spooky.

211. If you were to draw a long, thin line down the west coast of South America, that would be **Chile.** It's about **2,650 miles long,** which is much longer than the west coast of the United States. Chile is a special country because it has places like Easter Island, which is really far out in the Pacific Ocean. Chile also says that part of Antarctica belongs to them, which makes their country even bigger!

212. If you've heard of Chile, then you've probably heard of **Peru** too. Both countries are on the west coast of South America. Peru is also very long, about 1,500 miles. Peru is famous for the Incas, who were ancient people who built a really cool city called Machu Picchu high up in the Andes Mountains. Unlike Chile, Peru doesn't claim part of Antarctica, but it has a huge rainforest called the Amazon. Peru has all kinds of amazing places, from deserts to mountains.

213. Have you ever seen a mountain that looks like a rainbow? In Peru, there's a mountain called **Vinicunca, or the Rainbow Mountain.** It's really tall, about 17,000 feet high! The mountain is covered in stripes of different colors because of all the special minerals in the soil. It's a pretty new discovery, but it's already a very popular place to visit.

214. One of the coolest places in Chile is called **the Marble Caves.** They're located on a big lake called General Carrera, in a place called Patagonia. These caves are made of marble, and they're really, really old! The water has been carving them for thousands of years, and now they're these amazing blue and green colors. You can only get to them by boat, so it's like a little adventure to see them!

215. **Did you know that Africa and Russia are almost the same width?** That's right, they're both about 4,600 miles wide! It might look like Russia is much bigger on a map, but that's just a trick. Maps can be tricky because they make some places look bigger or smaller than they really are. Africa is a really big place with lots of different animals and people. It's just as wide as Russia and it's important to remember that when we look at maps.

3.1. Unusual phenomena

216. In warm seas, you can see the **glowing water,** when waves crash against the shore in the dark and flash with a bright light, and ships and fish leave glowing trails on the sea surface. This phenomenon occurs due to bioluminescence which is the ability of some marine organisms, such as plankton, jellyfish, and bacteria, to emit light. This glow is the result of a chemical reaction inside their cells and may be a way of protecting themselves or attracting their food.

Glowing sand on the beach is caused by the same bioluminescent organisms that are washed up on the shore by the waves. When you step on the sand or move it, these microorganisms react to the mechanical action and begin to glow, creating a magical glow under your feet.

Glowing snow can be seen in some parts of the world. It is most often caused by bioluminescent organisms, such as bacteria or microorganisms, living in snow masses.

Snow of unusual colors, such as red, green, or blue, is a rare phenomenon associated with the presence of algae or bacteria, such as snow algae which are microscopic organisms that live on the surface of snow and ice. They contain red pigments (such as astaxanthin) and give the snow a pink or reddish shade, known as watermelon snow. These algae are able to survive in extremely cold conditions and play an important role in mountain and polar ecosystems.

3.2. Water

217. If you look at a globe, you'll see that a lot of it is blue. That's because about **71% of the Earth is covered in water.** But most of that water is salty, like the water in the ocean. In fact, 97% of all the water on Earth is salty! 224. But even though water covers most of the Earth, it doesn't weigh very much. Water only makes up about **0.02% of the Earth's weight.** Most of the water is in the oceans, seas, and glaciers, but you can also find it in rivers, lakes, and underground.

218. **Only 3% of the Earth's water is freshwater,** and most of that (about 70%) is frozen in glaciers and ice caps.

219. Water is the only thing on Earth that can be **a solid (like ice), a liquid, or a gas (like steam),** and it can change between these states really easily.

220. Your body is mostly made of water! **About 60-70% of your body is water.** Water helps your body do everything it needs to do.

221. Water is really special because **when it freezes into ice, it actually gets bigger!** This makes ice lighter than water, so it floats.
230. On average, a person can only live for about **3 days without water.** That means water is even more important for life than food!

222. Every day, about **500,000 cubic kilometers of water move around the Earth** through evaporation and rain.

223. There's a special place in Azerbaijan called **Kergelan** where you can see water that burns! It's like magic! There's a little hole in the ground, and when water comes out, it catches on fire and burns with a blue flame. This happens because there's a special gas called methane mixed in with the water. It's really cool to see nature doing something so amazing!

3.3. Rivers and waterfalls

224. The longest rivers in the world:
Amazon - 4,345 miles, South America.
Nile - 4,258 miles, Africa.
Yangtze - 3,917 miles, China.

225. There's been a big debate about which river is longer, the Nile or the Amazon. For a long time, people thought the Nile was the longest at about 4,258 miles. But now, some scientists think the Amazon might be even longer, maybe up to 4,345 miles, if you count all its small beginnings.
It's hard to say for sure which river is longer because there are different ways to measure rivers. For example, it's tricky to find the exact starting point of the Amazon River. **So, depending on how you measure, either the Nile or the Amazon could be the longest!**

226. The Nile River flows through 11 different countries in Africa, like Egypt, Sudan, and Uganda. The Nile is actually made up of two big rivers, the White Nile and the Blue Nile, that come together in Sudan. A long time ago, the Nile was super important to the ancient Egyptians because it gave them water for their farms and helped their crops grow. Even today, the Nile is still really important for Egypt and Sudan because it gives them lots of water.

227. **The Amazon River** is in South America, and it might be the longest river in the world! It's about 4,345 miles long. The Amazon River also carries more water than any other river on Earth: about 20% of all the fresh water that goes into the ocean. The Amazon Rainforest is around

the river, and it's full of lots of different kinds of plants and animals that you can't find anywhere else.

228. The Amazon River is like a shape-shifter! Sometimes it's skinny, and other times it's super wide. During the dry season, it's usually between 1 and 6 miles across. But when it rains a lot, the Amazon River gets so big it can spread out up to 30 miles wide, turning into a huge, watery world!

229. The Amazon River didn't always flow the way it does now. Millions of years ago, it actually flowed **the opposite way**, from east to west, and went into the Pacific Ocean. But then, the Earth's crust moved around and created big mountains called the Andes. These mountains blocked the river, so it had to change its direction and started flowing east into the Atlantic Ocean.

230. **A tributary** is like a smaller river that flows into a bigger river. It adds water to the bigger river, but it doesn't go straight into the ocean.

231. **The Amazon River has more tributaries than any other river** in the world! It has over 200 tributaries.

232. **The Yangtze River** is the longest river in Asia. It runs through China, starting in the Tibetan Plateau and flowing into the East China Sea. The Yangtze River is very important to China because it provides water for millions of people and helps grow food. There's a big hydroelectric power plant on the river called the Three Gorges, which is the biggest in the world.

233. **One of the worst floods ever** was the 1931 flood in China. It flooded a lot of land near the Yangtze and Huang He rivers and killed

between 1 and 4 million people. Millions of homes were also destroyed. This flood is considered one of the deadliest disasters in history.

234. **Oxbow lakes are the lakes that are formed when a river changes its path and leaves behind a curved shape.** These lakes look like a horseshoe or a half-moon. Over time, they become separate from the river and form their own little lake. Oxbow lakes are usually shallow and are a great home for many kinds of fish and birds.

235. **The Mississippi River** is actually shorter than it used to be. A long time ago, people wanted to stop the river from flooding and make it easier for boats to travel on it. So, they changed the way the river flowed. They made the river straighter, which created many oxbow lakes. Because of these changes, the Mississippi River is now about **150 miles** shorter.

236. **The Ganges River** is one of the biggest rivers in Asia. It's about 1,680 miles long and flows through India and Bangladesh. The Ganges River makes a huge river delta, which is where a river splits into many smaller rivers before it flows into the ocean. This delta is very fertile, which means it's great for growing food. Hindus think the Ganges River is very special and holy, and it's important to millions of people.

237. **The Ob River** is one of the biggest rivers in Asia. It has about 150,000 smaller rivers flowing into it, called tributaries. All these tributaries give the Ob River lots of water and help make a big river system that provides water for all of Western Siberia. The Ob River flows north into the Kara Sea and makes one of the largest river basins in the world.

238. In Poland, there's an amazing place where **two rivers meet at a perfect right angle!** These rivers are called the Welna and the Nelba. What's even more amazing is that their waters don't mix together because they have different temperatures and flow at different speeds. Scientists

have even done an experiment with colored water: red water in the Welna and blue water in the Nelba. When they meet, the red water stays on its side and the blue water stays on its side, like magic!

239. **A waterfall** is formed when a river or stream flows over a very steep part of the land. This steep part can be a cliff or a big rock. Over many, many years, the water wears away the softer rocks underneath, making a big drop. This drop is where the waterfall happens! Waterfalls can be created by earthquakes, volcanoes, or simply by the water wearing away the land over a long time.

240. **Angel Falls** is the tallest waterfall in the world! It's a whopping 3,212 feet tall! You can find it in the rainforest of Venezuela, on a mountain called Auyantepui. When the water falls from so high, most of it turns into mist before it even hits the ground. The waterfall was named after a pilot named Jimmy Angel, who was the first person to tell the world about it in 1933.

241. **Niagara Falls** is a huge and very famous waterfall that's located where the United States and Canada meet. It's actually made up of three different waterfalls: the Horseshoe Falls, the American Falls, and the Bridal Veil Falls. The Horseshoe Falls is the biggest part. The entire waterfall is about 167 feet tall and almost 3,950 feet wide! Can you imagine how much water that is? Every second, about 85,000 cubic meters of water goes over the falls. It's not just a beautiful sight, it also helps to create electricity and millions of people visit it every year.

242. If you visit Paraguay, you should try to find the **Salto Cristal waterfalls.** They're like a hidden gem in the rainforest near the town of La Colmena. The water is so clear it looks like glass, and it falls about 150 feet into a beautiful pool. Around the pool, there are lots of green trees and big rocks.

3.4. Coastline

243. **Barrier islands** are special islands that are long and thin, and they run right along the coast. Imagine a long sandbar that protects the land from big ocean waves. These islands are made from sand that is moved by the ocean with its waves and currents. They're really important because they help protect the coast from being worn away. Also, many plants and animals live on barrier islands, making them important ecosystems.

244. The most famous barrier islands are:
Outer Banks, USA — located off the coast of North Carolina and Virginia. **Galveston**, USA — a barrier island off the coast of Texas. **Long Island**, USA — one of the largest barrier islands off the coast of New York. **Fraser Island**, Australia — the largest sand barrier island in the world. Barrier islands protect the coast from strong winds, waves, and tides.

245. A **cape** is a piece of land that sticks out into the ocean, lake, or river. It's like a point on a map. Capes can be big or small, and they're often used as landmarks. Capes are formed when the softer rocks around them get worn away by the water, leaving the harder rocks sticking out. A famous example is the **Cape of Good Hope** in South Africa.

246. **Cape Reinga is the highest point in New Zealand!** It's where you can see two big oceans, the Tasman Sea and the Pacific Ocean, meet. The waves from these oceans crash together and create a really cool foamy area. For the Maori people, the original people of New Zealand, Cape Reinga is a very special place.

247. **Big capes often have lighthouses on them.** Lighthouses help boats find their way when they're near the shore. Sometimes, the water near capes can be dangerous because of big waves, strong currents, or hidden rocks. Lighthouses have bright lights that can be seen from far away.

These lights warn sailors about the danger so they can safely go around it. For example, the lighthouse at Cape Hatteras in the United States helps boats avoid dangerous sandbanks.

248. **Coastline formations like caves, arches, and pillars are made by the ocean!** Waves crash against the rocks and slowly wear them away, making these cool shapes.

Caves are made when the waves dig into the rocks.

Arches are made when a cave gets so big that there's a hole all the way through.

Pillars are made when the top of an arch falls off, leaving a tall rock standing alone.

You can often find these formations on beaches with big waves and strong winds.

249. **The Twelve Apostles** are a group of tall rock formations, or pillars, along **the Great Ocean Road** in Australia. These limestone pillars were made by the ocean crashing against the cliffs. Even though they're called the Twelve Apostles, there are actually less than twelve now because some of them have fallen down over time.

250. **The Azure Window was a natural rock arch on the island of Gozo in Malta.** It was famous for its beautiful view of the Mediterranean Sea. Lots of people went to see it. But in 2017, the strong waves and wind from the sea made the rock too weak, and it collapsed.

251. **The Chesapeake Bay is a huge, watery maze where rivers meet the ocean.** It's a special place filled with cool sea creatures, yummy blue crabs, and lots of mysteries to explore. Every evening, the sunset makes the bay look really magical!

3.5. Seas and oceans

252. There are 5 oceans in total:
The Pacific Ocean is the largest one.
The Atlantic Ocean is the second largest.
The Indian Ocean is in the south of Asia.
The Southern Ocean is around Antarctica.
The Arctic Ocean is the smallest, in the north.

253. For a long time, people thought there were only **4 big oceans:** the Pacific, Atlantic, Indian, and Arctic Oceans. But in the year 2000, special ocean experts decided that there should be a fifth ocean! They called it **the Southern Ocean,** and it's the ocean that's all around Antarctica.

254. **The Pacific Ocean** is the largest ocean on Earth. It's huge! It's so big that it covers about **63 million square miles**. The Pacific Ocean is located between the continents of North and South America on one side, and Asia and Australia on the other. It's so big that it covers almost a third of our entire planet!

255. **The Atlantic Ocean** is the second biggest ocean in the world! It's about 41 million square miles. It separates the Americas from Europe and Africa. There's a special current in the Atlantic Ocean called the Gulf Stream. It's like a river inside the ocean, and it helps make the weather warmer in many countries.

256. **The Indian Ocean** is the third biggest ocean in the world! It's about 27 million square miles. It's located between Africa, Asia, Australia, and Antarctica. Many ships sail across the Indian Ocean to trade goods with different countries.

257. **The Southern Ocean is the newest ocean!** It was only made official in the year 2000. It surrounds Antarctica, the coldest place on Earth, and goes all the way down to 60 degrees south. The Southern Ocean is about 7.8 million square miles big. It's really important for our planet's weather because it helps control the ocean currents and the weather.

258. **The Arctic Ocean is the smallest and shallowest ocean on Earth.** It's about 5.4 million square miles big. This ocean is located around the North Pole and is covered in ice for most of the year. The ice in the Arctic Ocean changes with the seasons, but in recent years, it has been getting smaller because of global warming.

259. **All the oceans on Earth are connected** and make one global ocean. Water moves between the oceans through currents, like the Gulf Stream in the Atlantic and other currents in the Pacific and Indian Oceans. These ocean currents carry heat, food, and tiny living things, helping to keep our planet healthy and balanced.

260. **Point Nemo** is a special place in the Pacific Ocean. It's the farthest you can get from any land on Earth. The nearest islands are over 1,600 miles away! It's named after Captain Nemo, a character from a famous book. Fun fact: sometimes, astronauts in space are actually closer to Point Nemo than anyone on Earth!

261. In Sicily, Italy, there's a special **lake called the Stagno di Vendicari.** It's really salty, just like the famous Dead Sea. This salty lake is in a beautiful nature park. Because the water is so salty, it's really easy to float in it! It's almost like floating in a giant pool of salt water.

262. **Ocean currents are movements of water in the ocean.** They're caused by a few different things:

Wind: When the wind blows across the ocean, it pushes the water and creates surface currents.

Temperature and salt: Water that is warmer and has less salt in it is lighter, so it floats on top of colder, saltier water. This difference in weight creates deep currents.

The Earth's spin: Because the Earth spins, currents don't go in a straight line. They get pushed to the right in the Northern Hemisphere and to the left in the Southern Hemisphere.

263. **The Antarctic Circumpolar Current is like a giant river in the ocean.** It's the biggest and strongest one on Earth! This current flows all around Antarctica and connects the Atlantic, Pacific, and Indian Oceans. It carries a huge amount of water, more than any other current.

264. Imagine a really big wave, much bigger than the waves you see at the beach. **That's a tsunami!** Tsunamis are caused by big underwater earthquakes or volcanic eruptions. They can travel really fast across the ocean, and when they reach the shore, they can be over 100 feet tall! These giant waves can cause a lot of damage to coastal cities and towns.

265. The biggest tsunami ever happened on December 26, 2004, in the Indian Ocean. It was caused by a very big earthquake near Indonesia. The waves were over **100 feet tall!** They crashed into many countries, like Indonesia, Thailand, Sri Lanka, and India. Sadly, **over 230,000** people died. It was one of the worst natural disasters ever.

266. **The Mediterranean Sea is a huge inland sea.** It's surrounded by three continents: Europe, Asia, and Africa. Can you imagine how big that is? It's about **970,000 square miles**! The only way for water to flow in or out of the Mediterranean Sea is through a narrow passage called the Strait of Gibraltar. It connects the Mediterranean Sea to the Atlantic Ocean.

267. **The Caspian Sea** is the biggest lake in the world! Even though it's called a sea, it's actually a really big lake with salty water. It's about 143,000 square miles. It's located between Europe and Asia and touches the countries of Russia, Kazakhstan, Turkmenistan, Iran, and Azerbaijan.

268. **The Caribbean Sea** is home to a vast archipelago of over 7,000 islands. Some of these islands are quite large, like Cuba, Jamaica, and Puerto Rico, while others are tiny and remote. It's a stunning variety of islands, each with its own unique culture and natural beauty.

269. Can you imagine **the Mediterranean Sea all dried up?** Well, it almost happened millions of years ago! A long time ago, the strait of Gibraltar closed up, and the Mediterranean Sea was cut off from the Atlantic Ocean. With no water coming in, and the hot sun evaporating the water, the Mediterranean Sea almost completely dried up, leaving behind a giant salt flat. But then, something amazing happened, the strait opened up again, and the sea filled back up!

270. **Seawater is salty because of all the minerals that are dissolved in it.** Things like salt, or sodium chloride, get into the ocean from rocks and volcanoes. Over time, all this salt has made the ocean water salty. Think of a bathtub. When you wash your hands, the soap goes down the drain, right? It's kind of like that with rivers and oceans. The salt from the land washes into the ocean, just like the soap goes down the drain. So, the ocean gets salty, but **the rivers stay fresh.**

271. **The saltiest oceans are in the hottest places, but the least salty oceans are in the coldest places!** In the Arctic and Antarctic, the water is less salty because the ice that melts there is fresh water. It mixes with the salty ocean water, making it less salty.

272. **About 18,000 years ago, during the last Ice Age,** the sea level was about 400 feet lower than it is today. This happened because a lot of the Earth's water was frozen in giant glaciers.

3.6. Glaciers

273. Imagine a giant ice cube that's so heavy, it can slowly slide across the ground. That's a glacier! Glaciers are formed when snow piles up year after year and turns into ice. They can be found in cold places like the Arctic and Antarctica. Glaciers shape the land as they move.

274. Imagine the Earth putting on a big, icy coat. That's what happens during **an ice age!** It gets so cold that a lot of the planet is covered in thick sheets of ice. After an ice age, the Earth takes off its icy coat and it gets warmer. These warmer times are called interglacial periods.

275. Over the past **2.4 billion years**, our planet has gone through about **24 ice ages!**

276. You might think there's no ice near the equator, but that's not always true! Even in really hot places, you can find glaciers on tall mountains like **Kilimanjaro** in Africa and **the Andes** in South America. This is because the higher you go up a mountain, the colder it gets, so snow can pile up and turn into ice, even if you're close to the equator.

277. The biggest glacier outside the North and South Poles is called the **Siachen Glacier**. It's located in the Himalayas, a big mountain range between India and Pakistan. This glacier is about **47 miles** long, making it one of the largest mountain glaciers in the world!

278. The ice in Antarctica is really, really thick! On average, it's about **1.2 miles** thick, but in some places, it can be more than **3 miles** thick! It's the thickest ice on our whole planet.

279. **Glaciers move because of gravity.** They're so heavy that the ice at the bottom slowly squashes and flows like really thick honey. The ice at the top can move faster, and sometimes it cracks. As the glacier moves downhill, it carries rocks and dirt with it, leaving them behind when the ice melts.

280. Rocks that are left behind by glaciers are called **pellets** or **erratics**. These big, heavy rocks were carried by glaciers and dropped off in new places when the ice melted. They can be very different from the other rocks around them, which is a clue that they were brought there by a glacier.

281. The city of Okotoks in Canada got its name from the Blackfoot word **"okatok,"** which means "rock." This is because of a big rock, called the Okotoks Rock, that's near the city. The rock was left there by a glacier a long, long time ago. It's so special that it became a famous landmark in the area.

282. An **iceberg** is a huge piece of ice that breaks off from a glacier or ice shelf and floats in the ocean. About **90%** of an iceberg is hidden underwater, which makes them very dangerous for ships. The biggest icebergs are found in cold places like Antarctica and the Arctic.

283. **Some icebergs are so big, they're almost as big as a whole state!** For example, the A-68 iceberg that broke off from Antarctica was about the size of Delaware. Other icebergs can be as big as Rhode Island! These giant icebergs floating in the ocean remind us how powerful nature is and how amazing the polar regions are.

84

3.7. Continental movement, earthquakes, and volcanoes

284. In 1912, a scientist named Alfred Wegener came up with a really interesting idea. He thought that all the continents on Earth were once connected, forming a supercontinent called Pangaea. Over millions of years, these continents slowly moved apart, just like pieces of a puzzle. **This idea is called continental drift.** Scientists have since found lots of evidence to support Wegener's theory.

285. A long, long time ago, all the lands of the Earth were united into one giant supercontinent called **Pangaea.** This was about 335 million years ago! Over millions of years, this supercontinent started to break apart into smaller pieces, which eventually became the continents we know today. This happened because of the Earth's tectonic plates moving around.

286. The continents are still moving today! This is called **plate tectonics.** The continents float on giant pieces of the Earth's crust called tectonic plates. These plates move very slowly, just a few inches every year. When these plates bump into each other, it can cause earthquakes and mountains.

287. **Mountains are formed when the Earth's tectonic plates move and crash into each other.** Sometimes, one plate goes under the other, and sometimes they squeeze together and push the Earth's crust up. This process, called orogenesis, creates mountain ranges like the Himalayas. The Himalayas were formed when the Indian and Eurasian plates collided.

288. **The Himalayas are still growing!** They get taller by about 0.2-0.4 inches every year. This is because the Indian and Eurasian tectonic plates are still pushing against each other, making the mountains grow taller and taller.

289. **Switzerland is getting smaller!** It's shrinking by about 0.1 inch every year. At the same time, the Alps, the big mountains in Switzerland, are getting taller by about 0.04 to 0.06 inches every year. This is happening because Switzerland is in a special place where two big pieces of the Earth's crust are pushing against each other.

290. Did you know that Mount Everest isn't actually the highest point on Earth? There's **a volcano in Ecuador called Chimborazo** that's about 20,548 feet tall. It's not as tall as Everest above sea level, but its top is actually farther away from the center of the Earth. That's because the Earth is a bit like a squishy ball. It bulges out at the middle (the equator), and Chimborazo is closer to the middle. So, even though it's not the tallest mountain if you measure from sea level, it's the farthest away from the center of the Earth!

291. **Japan is a very mountainous country.** About 80% of it is covered in mountains! Some of the most famous mountains are Mount Fuji, Tateyama, and Hakusan. Mountains are very important in Japanese culture and religion, especially Mount Fuji which is considered to be very special. Even though Japan has so many mountains, it also has big, busy cities and beautiful coastlines.

292. In Indonesia, on the island of Java, there's **a volcano called Ijen.** It's famous for its blue fire and a very special lake that's full of acid! The volcano spews out gases that are full of sulfur, and when these gases come out, they catch on fire and create a beautiful blue light. The lake in the volcano's crater is the biggest acid lake in the world and it's a bright turquoise color. It makes the whole place look like something from a fairy tale.

293. **Earthquakes are sudden shaking of the ground.** They happen when the giant pieces of the Earth's crust, called tectonic plates, move and bump into each other. This movement releases a lot of energy, which creates seismic waves. These waves travel through the Earth and cause the ground to shake.

294. **The Richter scale** is used to measure how strong an earthquake is. The higher the number on the scale, the stronger the earthquake. Each number is a lot bigger than the number before it.

295. In Turkmenistan, there's a place called the **"Gates of Hell."** It's a big hole in the ground that's always on fire! A long time ago, in 1971, people were digging for gas when they accidentally made this big hole. To stop the gas from coming out, they set it on fire. They thought the fire would go out quickly, but it's been burning for over 50 years! It looks really cool at night, but it's also a bit scary.

296. Japan had a huge earthquake in 2011. It was so powerful, it measured **9.0** on the Richter scale. This earthquake caused a huge tsunami that swept across the land, destroying many towns and cities. Unfortunately, a nuclear power plant called **Fukushima** was also damaged, causing a serious problem. This disaster took the lives of about **16,000** people and is considered one of the worst natural disasters in recent history.

297. **In 1906, a really big earthquake happened in San Francisco. It was so strong, it was a magnitude 7.9!** After the earthquake, there were huge fires that burned for days. Sadly, about 3,000 people died. The city was almost completely destroyed and had to be rebuilt.

298. Can you imagine the biggest shake you've ever felt? Well, **the earthquake in Alaska in 1964 was a million times bigger!** It was so strong, it was a 9.2 on the Richter scale. The earthquake caused giant waves that crashed into the land and caused a lot of damage. Over 130 people lost their lives.

299. **The most devastating earthquake in history happened in Shaanxi province, China, in 1556.** It was so powerful that it killed around 830,000 people. This is more than the population of a large city! The earthquake caused widespread destruction and is considered the deadliest natural disaster in recorded history.

300. Volcanoes and mountains are different because of how they're made. **Volcanoes are made from hot, melted rock** called magma that comes up from deep inside the Earth and cools to form a pointy shape. **Mountains, on the other hand, are made when the Earth's crust gets pushed together or worn away over time.** They don't have any magma or lava.

301. In 1883, there was a huge volcano eruption in Indonesia called **Krakatoa.** It was so loud that people could hear it from 3,000 miles away! The explosion caused giant waves called tsunamis that destroyed many towns and villages. Over 36,000 people lost their lives. The ash from the volcano went way up into the sky and made the whole world a little bit colder for a while.

302. In 1815, a volcano called Tambora erupted in Indonesia. It was one of the biggest volcanic eruptions ever! It was so powerful that it threw a huge amount of ash and gas into the sky. This caused a **"year without a summer" in 1816.** The Earth's temperature dropped, and crops failed in many parts of the world, including Europe and North America. The lack of food led to widespread famine and the deaths of thousands of people.

303. A long time ago, in **1667**, there was a terrible earthquake in the city of Dubrovnik. It was one of the strongest earthquakes ever recorded in that area. The earthquake was so powerful that it caused widespread damage. Many of the city's historic buildings, including palaces and churches, were completely destroyed. It's estimated that between 3,000 and 5,000 people lost their lives in the disaster. After the earthquake, the people of Dubrovnik had to rebuild their city from almost nothing.

4. The Human
4.1. The Earth population

304. The population of the Earth in 2024 is estimated to be around **8 billion people**.

305. **The Black Death (the bubonic plague)** was a very serious disease that happened in the 1300s. It spread all over Europe and killed a huge number of people. **Between 30% and 60%** of the people in Europe died from the Black Death. Some people think that as many as 75 - 200 million people died worldwide. It was one of the worst disasters ever.

306. **Asia is the most crowded continent.** Over 4.7 billion people live there! That's almost 60% of all the people on Earth!

307. **Antarctica** is the emptiest continent. There are no people who live there all year round. Only about **1,000** to **5,000** people live there at a time, and they're scientists who work at special research stations.

308. When a place like a city or a country is crowded with lots of people, we say it's **densely populated.** That means there are a lot of people living in a small area.

309. **Manila**, the capital of the Philippines, is known for being the most densely populated city in the world. That means there are a lot more people living there than in other cities. It's so crowded that there are around 119,600 people per square mile.

310. **Monaco** is a tiny country located on the Mediterranean Sea. Even though it's very small, it's home to a lot of people. In fact, it's the most densely populated country in the world. That means there are about 49,000 people living in every square mile. It's like a big city squeezed into a very small space.

311. **Tristan da Cunha** is the loneliest place in the world! It's a group of islands way out in the middle of the South Atlantic Ocean. The nearest land is over **1,200 miles away**! Can you believe that only about **270 people** live there? It's like being on your own private island!

312. The highest city in the world is **La Rinconada** in Peru that's located in the Andes mountains. It's really high up in the mountains, about **16,700 feet** above sea level! People live there and mine for gold, even though it's a very tough place to live.

313. If you look at how many crimes happen for each person, **Vatican City** sometimes has a lot. This is because so many people visit, but not very many people live there. All those visitors can make the crime numbers go up, especially for little things like stealing.

314. When it comes to really serious crimes, like people killing each other, **Caracas**, the capital of Venezuela, is at the top of the list. There are many reasons for this. The country has been facing a lot of problems, such as not having enough money and political disagreements. These problems have led to a lot of violence, and there aren't enough police officers to keep everyone safe.

4.2. Human Body

315. Did you know that **your body is mostly water? About 60%** of your body is made up of water! So, if a person weighs 154 pounds, about 92 pounds of that is water!

316. **All the parts inside your body work together to keep you alive.** For example, your heart is like a pump that moves blood around your body. And your lungs help you breathe and get oxygen. Cool fact: your liver does over 500 jobs including cleaning your blood and storing energy.

317. Inside your stomach, there's a very **strong acid that helps break down the food** you eat. It's so strong it can even dissolve metal! But your stomach has a special lining that protects it from this acid. And even though this lining gets worn down, your body is always making new cells to replace it.

318. **The small intestine** is part of your digestive system. It's a long, narrow tube that helps break down food. If you could stretch it out, it would be about 20 feet long! That's longer than a giraffe's neck!

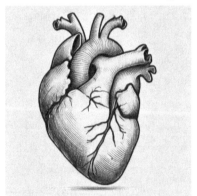

319. Your heart is a muscle that pumps blood to every part of your body. **An adult's heart** is about the size of your fist and weighs around 10 ounces. That's about as much as a can of soda! Every day, your heart works hard to pump about 2,000 gallons of blood. That's like filling a small pool!

320. **Grown-ups have 206 bones** in their bodies. And the smallest bone is in your ear! It's tiny, only about as long as a grain of rice!

321. Your **skin** is actually the biggest organ in your body! If you could spread it out flat, it would be almost about as big as a bed!

322. **Your brain is like a supercomputer** inside your head. It weighs about the same as a small laptop and it's in charge of everything you do, from thinking to playing games.

323. When you feel sleepy or bored, your brain needs more oxygen. **Yawning** is your body's way of getting more air. It helps to cool down your brain and make you feel more alert.

324. When you **sleep**, your body and brain get a chance to rest and repair. While you sleep, your brain sorts out all the things you learned that day, and your body cells get a chance to grow. If you don't get enough sleep, you'll feel tired and won't be able to think or move very well.

325. **Sleep** is really important for our bodies and brains. You can go without sleep for about 2-3 days, but it's really bad for you! If you don't get enough sleep, your brain and body won't work as well. After about 24 hours without sleep, you might find it hard to focus, and remember things, and you might feel more irritable.

326. **The record for staying awake the longest is 11 days**, but it's really dangerous. Your body needs sleep to function properly. If you don't get enough sleep, you can get really sick.

327. **The tallest person who ever lived** was Robert Wadlow from the United States. He was 8 feet 11 inches tall! Even when he died in 1940, he was still growing because of a special part of his body called the pituitary gland. This condition is called gigantism.

328. Chandra Bahadur Dangi, a man from Nepal, was **the shortest adult person** ever recorded. He was only 21.5 inches tall! In 2012, he was officially recognized as the shortest person in the world.

329. Can you imagine being as heavy as a small car? Jon Brower Minnoch was! He was **the heaviest person** ever recorded, weighing 1,400 pounds back in 1978.

330. Lucita Zarate, a famous actress from Mexico, was **the lightest adult woman** ever recorded. At just 24 inches tall and weighing only 4.7 pounds, she was incredibly tiny.

331. Humans can be really tough and can run for a very long time! For example, **Dean Karnazes is a super runner who once ran 350 miles without stopping for 80 hours straight**! He's famous for running really long distances and shows us that our bodies can do amazing things if we train hard.

332. **Usain Bolt holds the world record for the 100-meter sprint.** He set this record in 2009 when he ran 100 meters in just 9.58 seconds. That's incredibly fast! At his top speed, he was running at a speed of 27.8 miles per hour.

333. **One of the oldest people who ever lived** was a Japanese woman named Kane Tanaka. She was born in 1903 and lived to be **117 years old!** That's amazing! She loved playing games and eating sweets, and she was always happy. Kane Tanaka is a great example of how being positive and having fun can help you live a long life.

334. Can you believe that all the veins in your body put together are about **62,000 miles long?** That's like going around the Earth more than twice! Scientists figured this out a long time ago, in the 1800s. Veins are like tiny roads that carry blood back to your heart, bringing oxygen and food to all your body parts.

4.3. Subway, trains, and airplanes

335. The London Underground, which opened in 1863, was the first subway in the world. Today, it has 11 lines and is over 250 miles long, making it one of the biggest transportation systems in the world. 337. Shanghai in China has **the biggest subway** system in the world. It opened in 1993 and has grown a lot since then. With over 497 miles of tracks and 18 different lines, it's like a giant underground city! Every day, more than 10 million people use it to get around.

337. The New York City subway is one of the oldest and biggest subways in the world. It opened in 1904 and has been a major part of New York City ever since. With over 660 miles of tracks, it's a huge network that helps millions of people get around the city every day.

338. The New York City subway carries over **5 million people** every day! It runs 24 hours a day, all year long.

339. When we talk about **the longest subways** in the world, we usually mean the parts that people actually ride on. If we do that, the Shanghai Subway is the winner with over 500 miles of tracks. The New York City subway has a lot of tracks too, but some of them are used for things like cleaning the trains or moving them around when they're not carrying passengers.

340. One of the biggest subways in the world is in Shanghai, China. It's over 500 miles long, which makes it the longest subway in the world! It has 18 different lines and carries more than 10 million people every day!

341. The Tokyo subway is one of the busiest in the world. During rush hour, the trains can get so crowded that special people called oshiya help push people into the train so the doors can close. Over **8 million people** ride the Tokyo subway every day!

342. The deepest subway station in the whole world is located in Kyiv, Ukraine. It's called "Arsenalna" and it's about 346 feet underground! That's like being in a very tall building but under the ground! The station was built in 1960 and it's so deep because of the special kind of land where it is.

343. In Turin, Italy, there's **a subway called the Metro. It's one of the shortest subways** in the world, only about 4.5 miles long. The cool thing about it is that it doesn't need train drivers because it's completely automatic. The trains can start and stop all by themselves.

344. In the early 1600s, people in Britain started building railways where wagons were pulled along by horses. These were called **wagonways** and they were the beginning of railroads. But everything changed in 1825 when George Stephenson built the first steam railway called **the Stockton and Darlington Railway**. This steam train was faster and more powerful than horses, and it changed transportation forever.

345. The first railway that carried people opened in 1830 between **Liverpool and Manchester** in England. These trains were powered by steam engines and ran on a schedule, just like buses do today. This was a huge breakthrough in transportation. Soon, railways were being built all over the world, including the United States. In 1869, they finished building the first transcontinental railroad in the US, connecting the eastern and western parts of the country.

346. In 1869, a big dream came true for the United States. They finished building **the first railroad** that went all the way from the East Coast to the West Coast. It took six years of hard work, starting in 1863. This railroad was like a giant bridge that connected the different parts of the country. To celebrate, they drove a golden pin into the ground where the two sides of the railroad met in Utah. It was a symbol of the country coming together as one.

347. The United States is the home of one of the greatest inventions ever: the airplane. In 1903, two brothers named Wright flew the first-ever plane, **the Flyer**, over Kitty Hawk, North Carolina. This was a huge deal because it showed that humans could fly! Their invention started a new era of air travel, and it changed the way people travel and see the world.

348. The United States is the biggest player in the world when it comes to building airplanes. Companies like Boeing make huge planes that fly all over the world. Places like Atlanta's Hartsfield-Jackson Airport are so busy, it's like a city that never sleeps, with millions of people coming and going every year.

349. **The first time anyone ever flew across the Atlantic Ocean was in 1919.** Two British pilots named John Alcock and Arthur Brown made this amazing journey in a big plane called a Vickers Vimy. They flew from Newfoundland, Canada, to Ireland and it took them 16 hours. This flight was a huge deal because it opened up a whole new world of travel. People could now fly to places they could never go before!

350. **Over the past 100 years, flying on airplanes has changed a lot:** Technologies: Old airplanes were really different from the ones we fly on today. They were slow and not very comfortable. But now, we have amazing planes like the Boeing 787 and Airbus A350. They're fast, and quiet, and use special technology to make flying smooth and safe.

Comfort and convenience: Flying used to be pretty basic, but now airplanes are like flying hotels! You can get Wi-Fi, watch movies, get a snack or a meal, and sit in really comfy seats. **Availability:** A long time ago, only rich people could fly on airplanes. But now, flying is much more common!

There are lots of airlines with cheaper tickets, and you can fly to more places than ever before.
Safety: Flying is much safer now than it used to be. Airplanes have lots of safety rules. For example, they check your bags and ID before you get on the plane.
Global network: Airplanes have made the world a much smaller place. You can fly from one country to another in just a few hours. It's amazing how easy it is to travel to different places now!
Environmental compatibility: Airplanes today are being built in a way that's better for the environment. They use special engines that burn less fuel and are made with lighter materials, so they don't pollute the air as much.

4.4. History of Humanity

351. For most of human history, before there were farms and cities, **people used to hunt animals and gather plants for food.** This way of life lasted for a really long time! But around 12,000 years ago, people started farming, and everything changed. This is called the Neolithic Revolution.

352. Long, long ago, a Viking explorer named Erik the Red was looking for a new place to live. After being kicked out of Iceland, he sailed west and found a giant island covered in ice. But he had a clever idea! To make the island sound more appealing, **he named it Greenland, even though it wasn't very green at all.**

353. **Persia** is the old name for the country we know as Iran today. Even though people started calling it **Iran** a long time ago, the official name didn't change until 1935.

354.Can you believe that one of the **first mail services** was started in Persia around **500 B.C.** by a king named Darius? He created a system where riders on horses carried messages between different stations. This system was so good that people back then used to say, "Neither snow nor rain nor heat nor gloom of night can prevent couriers from the swift completion of their appointed rounds."

355. **Paper money** has a long history, and it all started in China! Chinese people started using paper money during the Tang Dynasty, which was a long time ago. By the 11th century, when the Song Dynasty was in power, paper money was a normal part of everyday life. The government recognized it as a real form of money.

356. England, as we know it today, was officially created in 927. That's when King Athelstan joined many smaller kingdoms together to make one big kingdom. Before that, England was made up of lots of little kingdoms like Wessex, Mercia, and Northumbria.

357. **King Henry VIII** was a king of England who had **six wives** and made a big change to the church. He wanted to marry Anne Boleyn, but the Catholic Church wouldn't let him divorce his first wife. So, he started his own church in England, called **the Church of England**.

358. **Queen Elizabeth I,** the daughter of King Henry VIII and Anne Boleyn, ruled England for many years. She was known as the "Virgin Queen" because she never married. Her reign, from 1558 to 1603, was a golden age for England. It was a time of great exploration, wealth, and cultural achievements. This period is often referred to as the Elizabethan era, and it's when William Shakespeare wrote his famous plays.

359. **Christopher Columbus** was a famous explorer who sailed across the ocean in 1492. He was looking for a shorter route to Asia, he thought he had reached Asia, but he actually found a whole new world! People call it the New World, and it's made up of places like North and South America. His trip changed the world forever.

360. Believe it or not, Vikings from Scandinavia made it to North America centuries before Christopher Columbus! Around the year **1000**, a Norse explorer named **Leif Erikson** and his crew established a settlement in a region they called **Vinland**, which is thought to be somewhere near modern-day Newfoundland. However, unlike Columbus's discovery, the Vikings' settlement didn't lead to sustained European contact with the Americas.

361. **The Thirty Years' War** was a really big and bad war that happened in Europe from 1618 to 1648. It started because of a religious argument between Catholics and Protestants. But it quickly turned into a big fight over who was in charge. Many countries got involved, and **millions of people died.** The Treaty of Westphalia, which ended the war, redrew the map of Europe and established a new balance of power.

362. The first European to see **New Zealand** was a Dutch explorer named **Abel Tasman in 1642.** He sailed to New Zealand but didn't go on land because the Maori people who lived there weren't friendly. Later, in **1769,** a British explorer named **James Cook** came to New Zealand and made maps of the coastline. That's when more people in Europe started to know about New Zealand.

363. **Chocolate** was invented a long, long time ago by the ancient Maya and Aztec people in Central America. They made a special drink from cocoa beans. It was very bitter, and they used it in special ceremonies. When the Spanish people came to America, they brought chocolate back to Europe, and over time, it became the sweet treat we know today.

364. Before Alexander Fleming **discovered penicillin in 1928,** many people died from infections. Penicillin is an antibiotic that can fight bacteria, the tiny germs that cause infections. This discovery was a huge breakthrough in medicine and has saved countless lives.

365. **Vaccines** are like superheroes that help us fight germs. The first vaccine was made by Dr. Edward Jenner in 1796 to protect people from smallpox. This was a huge breakthrough in medicine, and it's the reason we have so many vaccines today. Vaccines help keep us safe and healthy.

Leave the review

As an independent author with a small marketing budget, reviews are my livelihood on this platform. If you enjoyed this book, I'd really appreciate it if you left your honest feedback on Amazon.

I love hearing from my readers and I personally read every single review.

Made in United States
Troutdale, OR
05/05/2025

31113115R00060